DK

A DORLING KINDERSLEY BOOK

Art Editor and Jacket Design
Claire Penny

US Editor
Constance Robinson

Production
Jo Rooke

Additional Photography
Dave King and Andy Crawford

Educational Consultant
Jane Bunting

Published in Canada by
Scholastic Canada Ltd.,
175 Hillmount Road, Markham, Ontario L6C IZ7
2 4 6 8 10 9 7 5 3 1

Canadian Cataloguing in Publication Data
Hanly, Sheila
Toddler's book of fun things to do
ISBN 0-590-51446-6

1. Toddlers – Juvenile literature. 2. Amusements – Juvenile literature.
3. Picture books for children. I. Shott, Stephen. II. Title.

HQ781.5.H36 1999   j305.232   C98-932469-9

Colour reproduction by Colourscan, Singapore
Printed and bound in Italy by L.E.G.O.

Dorling Kindersley would like to thank **Boden** for the loan of children's
clothes, and the following who were photographed for this book:
Charlotte Andiyapan, Blake Arthur, Peter Baskett,
Elliot Bell, Lucy Boswell, Adam Chand, Brooke Cheeseman,
Valentia Costa, Millie Dave, Edward Davison, Lucy Day,
Ian Fane, Evan Fiddy, Poppy Frean, Stephanie Galinsky,
Rebecca Glancy, Madeline Godfrey, Gus Gordon, Dojvan Harris,
Emma Humpston, Miles Kotey, Daniella Lambert, Courtney Lee-Smith,
Sammie Liu, Alex Mackenzie, Casey Mahadeo, Tanya Maxwell,
Amy McColgan, Duncan McGuinness, Tyler Meads, Gabi Mendel,
Pui Ming Chow, Finn Moore, Grace Moore, Shireen Nelson-Williams,
Lyam O'Connor, Louis Olmi, Marysia Olmi, Ayame Ponder,
Shannon Porter, Maddie Rakic Platt, Jade Rawlinson,
Suzanne Rawlinson, Ruth Sellers-Nixon, Amber Strauss,
Piers Tilbury, Michiko Vidal-Newman, Billie and
Joe Wackrill, Oliver Westcombe, Austin White,
Jemma Wilkinson, and Felix Yanez.

Toddler's Book of Fun Things to Do

Written by Sheila Hanly
Photography by Steve Shott

Scholastic Canada Ltd.

Note to parents

This book is packed with games and activities for you to share with your child, and also presents a wealth of early learning opportunities. As you look at the book together, encourage your child to copy the actions, play the games, and sing the songs. You can talk about the colors and shapes you see on the pages, and play counting games to reinforce number skills. Ask your child how certain objects would feel to touch – sticky cookie dough or a soft, fluffy toy – and to think about and copy the noises different things make – a ringing telephone or wailing fire engine. As you read the book with children, encourage them to talk about what they already know about the things pictured on each page and help them make links with their own experience. In the **Toddler's Book of Fun Things to Do,** you will find lots of inspiration and material to keep toddlers busy, interested, and entertained as they take their first steps on the road to discovery and learning.

Toddlers are energetic and, as every parent knows, they should not
be left unattended. Care should be taken when toddlers are using
equipment, playing near water, or performing exercises.

Contents

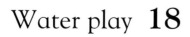

Good morning!

str-e-tch

A big stretch.

Potty time.

Wash your face.

Put on your shirt.

Slip on a sock.

Button up those overalls.

Let's have a good morning hug.

Brush your teeth . . . and brush your hair.

Now, get your doll dressed, too.

One, two, buckle your shoe.

Hands, knees, toes . . .

Scurry along like a crab.   Clap your hands.   Do a somersault.

Touch your head . . . your shoulders . . . your knees . . . and your toes.

Make a funny face.   Rub your tummy, pat your head.   Balance on one leg.

Point to your eyes . . .   and ears . . .   and mouth . . .   and nose.

Let's play together

Have a pillow fight.

Let's play tag.   You can't catch me!

Take giant steps.

Fly like an airplane.

Let's play follow the leader. Put your hands in the air.

1
2
3
4
5...

I'm hiding.

Counting to ten . . .
coming, ready or not!

13

Let's pretend

r-r-r-a-h-r-r
r-r-r-a-h-r-

Your teddy bear's sick. Make him all better.

Be a firefighter with a big, red fire engine.

Make us laugh, funny clown.

Clomp
Clomp
Clomp

Dress up like a grown-up.

Twist and twirl like a little ballerina.

I'm a wild cat.   I creep along . . .   and pounce!   Hear me **roar.**

My favorite toys

Make a giant
jigsaw puzzle.

Ring
Ring
Ring

Call a friend on
the telephone.

Kick . . .

and bounce . . .

and throw a ball.

Come on, ducks.

Time for a walk.

Off we go!

Build a long, low wall.

Toot
Toot

Drive a choo-choo train.

Water play

Make messy
mud pies.

Can you catch a raindrop?

Stamp in
a puddle.

splish splosh

Pour some water.

Make waves with
your hands.

Water the
flowers.

splash!

Make a
big splash.

...ding along

Rock back and
forth on a
rocking horse.

Have a
shoulder ride.

Giddy-ap, horsey.

Drive the car.

Have a race. Ready, set, go!

Hold on tight!

Push the cart.

Summer vacation

Help to pack the suitcase.

Put on a hat and sunglasses.

Dab on some sunscreen.

Lick a drippy ice cream cone.

Have a picnic.

22

Pack the teddy bear's clothes . . .   and close the bag.   All ready to go.

Draw circles
in the sand.

Listen to the
sea in a shell.

Build a giant sand castle.

Party time

Play "Pass the Parcel."

It's your turn now.

Listen to the music. Hold hands and dance around.

A game of musical chairs.

Let's do the conga!

Blow a little horn.

Pin the tail on the donkey.

Action songs

I'm a little teapot,

Short and stout.

Here is my handle,

Here is my spout.

When I get all steamed up,

Then I shout!

Tip me over,

And pour me out!

Anonymous

As **big** as a house.

As small as a mouse.

As **thin** as a pin.

As **wide** as a bridge.

Anonymous

27

Counting

1 One little teddy bear stands up straight.

2 Two little teddy bears make a gate.

3 Three little teddy bears sit in a ring.

5 Five little teddy bears make a noise.

4 Four little teddy bears bow to the king.

6 Six little teddy bears play with toys.

7 Seven little teddy bears stretch up high.

9 Nine little teddy bears dance all day.

8 Eight little teddy bears pretend to fly.

10 Ten little teddy bears hide away.

Adaptation of "Ten Little Teddy Bears" – Anonymous

Making pictures

Paint with your fingers.   Print with your hands. Now, try with your feet

Print with sponges – a star and a square.   Draw a picture with crayons.

Dab on bright
colors with a brush.

What sticky
paint!

33

Cleaning up

Straighten up the toy box.

Put away the books.

Switch on the vacuum cleaner.

Now, get that carpet clean.

At-choo! This needs dusting.

Clean up with a dustpan and brush.

Sweep the floor
with a broom.

Wash your doll's clothes.

In the kitchen

Help wash
the dishes.

Wipe the mug to get it dry.

Cut out a cookie shape.

Give the cake mix
a good stir.

In the bath

Sail a boat on a bubbly sea.

Scrub your nails
with a nailbrush.

Blow some foamy bubbles.

Now, wash your doll, too.

Bedtime

Give your doll
a hug and say,
"Night, night."

Let's read a story.

Put your teddy bear to bed.

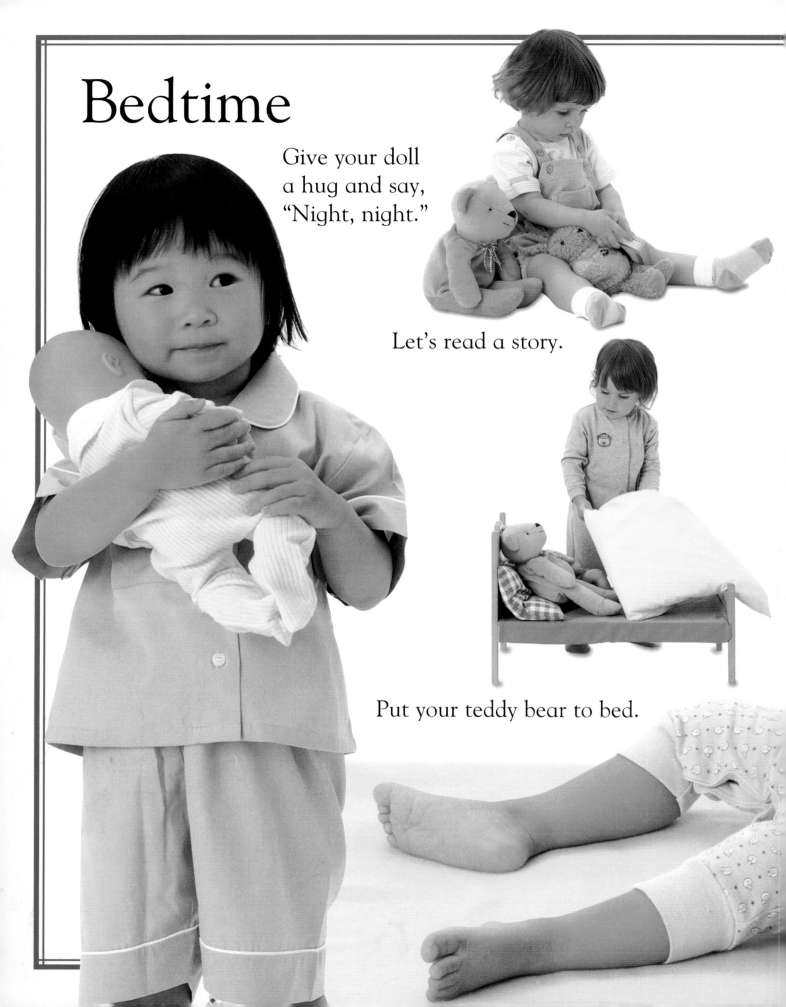

Where shall we begin?

Do you like this picture?

A big kiss
good night.

Sweet
dreams

Colors

Yellow
Play with the **yellow** toy ducks.

Orange
Suck on the **orange** orange.

Red
Drink from a **red** mug.

Green
Say "Hello" to the **green** frog.

Blue
Eat out of a **blue** bowl.

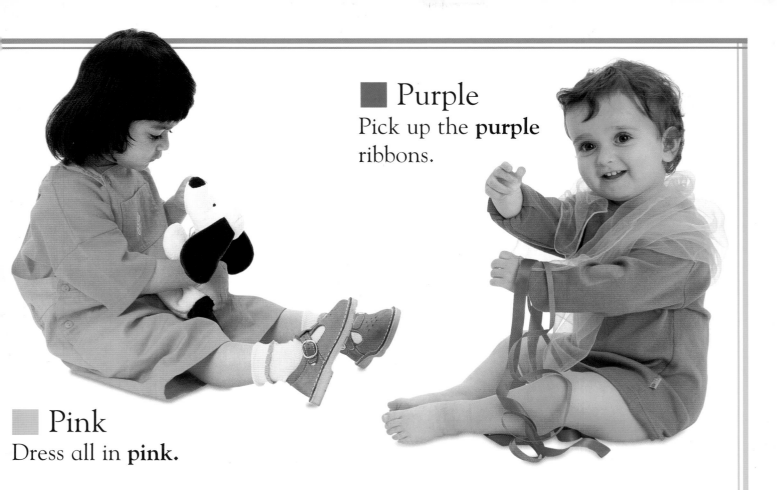

■ Purple
Pick up the **purple** ribbons.

■ Pink
Dress all in **pink.**

■ Brown
Meet a **brown** teddy bear.

■□ Black-and-white
Hug a **black-** and-**white** spotted dog.

Numbers

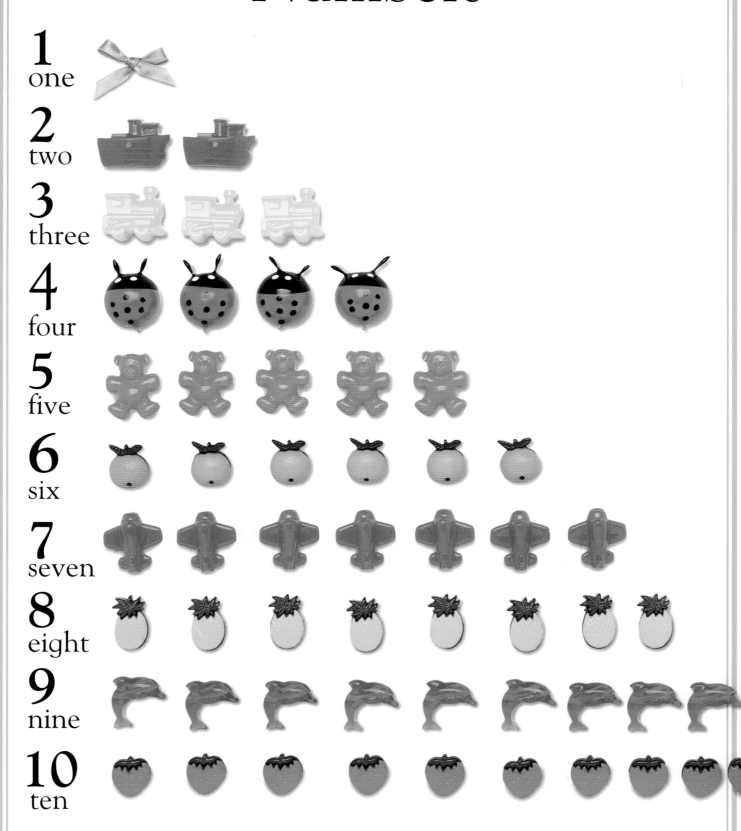

1 one

2 two

3 three

4 four

5 five

6 six

7 seven

8 eight

9 nine

10 ten

Word List

bag, 23	ducks, 17, 42	shell, 23
ball, 16	fire engine, 14	shirt, 8
bed, 40	flowers, 19	shoe, 9
boat, 38	frog, 42	sock, 8
books, 34	hat, 22	sponge, 8, 32
bowl, 42	house, 27	suitcase, 22
broom, 35	ice cream cone, 22	sunglasses, 22
brush, 9, 33, 35, 38	jigsaw puzzle, 16	teddy bear, 14, 23,
car, 21	mug, 36, 42	28–31, 40, 43
cart, 21	nailbrush, 38	telephone, 16
chairs, 25	orange, 42	train, 17
crayons, 32	potty, 8	vacuum
dog, 43	rocking horse, 20	cleaner, 34
doll, 9, 35, 39, 40	sand castle, 23	wall, 17

Word List Game

The list above contains many of the familiar, everyday objects that can be found in the **Toddler's Book of Fun Things to Do**. Use the list to help you find objects in the book and play a version of "I Spy" with your child. Choose an object and find the page on which it appears. Ask your child to find the object first and then talk together about your child's own experience of it. You might ask questions such as: "Do you have one of these? What is yours like? Is it the same as this one? How is it different? What do you like doing with yours?" Talk like this encourages young children to look more closely at the world around them and to think and talk about the things they see.